For Marlies

and the members of the

Sipplingen English Discussion Group

CONTENTS

INTRODUCTION

The idea for this small book came from reading the *How to be British* series, which explains the idiosyncrasies of the British in a humorous way, accompanied by suitable cartoons.

Although I was born and grew up in England, I have now lived in Germany for most of my life. Over the years I have gradually become integrated into German life but I can still appreciate how strange many things in this country may seem to foreigners. I have the feeling that when I am in Germany, my whole being becomes about 80% German and life seems quite normal. When I visit Britain, it takes about 24 hours for my British soul to be reawakened and for me to find life there quite normal too. In some respects, it is as if I have similarities to Jekyll and Hyde!

English is spoken all over the world and, in learning English, most people will also have learnt a lot about British life before ever visiting Britain. By contrast, far fewer people learn German and, as a result, most foreigners have little idea of German life until they visit the country. Particularly for those who come to Germany to study or work, it often comes as a shock to realise how different life is here to many other countries. The purpose of this book is to explain the idiosyncrasies of German life in a humorous way, which involves exaggerating some of the things that seem odd to foreigners.

Germany is made up of 16 Federal States and a multitude of different dialects, traditions, food and drink. This book is, therefore, *per se,* full of generalisations, as well as slight exaggerations, but I hope it will give the reader a feeling for life in Germany, accompanied by some giggles.

I am very grateful to many people for their assistance in producing this book. One of my first tasks in producing this book was to find somebody to draw the cartoons. Having no experience in such matters, I searched the internet and at second attempt found an excellent cartoonist, Hannes Mercker. Hannes is based in the Black Forest only about 100 kilometres from Lake Constance, where I live, but it was not until all the cartoons had been drawn that I met him for the first time. It is a fallacy to think that Germans have no humour but I am sure that some Germans would not feel too happy drawing cartoons making fun of their country. Hannes took it all in good humour befitting a cartoonist and working together with him has been a great pleasure.

The members of our English Discussion Group gave me general encouragement to write the book and four of the group gave up a lot of their time helping me. In particular, Benno Beck provided me with some of the ideas for the book and was an indispensable sounding board for my own ideas. Teresa Droxner assisted me by checking the draft chapters, both factually and grammatically, as I wrote them and also added some new ideas. Ann and David Sherwood not only carried out the boring proof-reading of the final version but also came up with numerous improvements to my rusty English.

Finally, every author needs encouragement and moral support from time to time and my wife, Marlies, provided that in great quantities. She has had some 48 years to become accustomed to life with a converted Brit and has learned that in my case it is really true that the way to a man is through his stomach! She not only kept my stomach in great shape by her delicious Anglo-German cooking but also kept me motivated when I had doubts whether anyone would appreciate my ideas of humour.

I hope the reader will learn much that he or she didn't already know about Germany from reading this book, while also having a good chuckle from time to time. I also hope that my many German friends and relatives will forgive me for telling the world about some aspects of life in Germany that seem very odd to people visiting the country for the first time. In fact, some aspects of life here still seem slightly strange to me after more than 40 years but they don't stop Germany from being a wonderful place to live, with beautiful countryside of all types, from the flat plains in the north to the high mountains in the south and from fertile farmland to huge forests. The country also has many wonderful historic towns and cities, despite the destruction that took place during the Second World War. I have never experienced any disadvantages because of my nationality, no doubt because the Germans and Brits generally have similar mentalities.

Once one can forget the very guttural and harsh-sounding aspects of the language, one will find that German can be very poetic and rich in expressions. Last but not least, once one has had daily interaction with Germans, one learns that it is a great exception if they are not friendly and welcoming.

John Morgan

Sipplingen, Germany

February 2020

1 A CONVERTED BRIT

Hello and guten Tag! As you may have gathered from the Introduction, I am the first product of a new species named *Homo Germanus Britannicus!* Having been born in England in 1938 and experienced the Second World War, I never thought I would be happy living in Germany one day. However, falling in love with a German girl changed my views on Germans and Germany completely.

After moving to Zurich in 1969 as the European Director of Real Estate and Construction of a large US corporation, I moved on to Germany three years later to become the managing director of the German subsidiary of an international property development group. My conversion now really gained momentum, since German soon became both my family and business language. Having a German wife and four children made it easy to make friends with other parents and the neighbours, whilst my work resulted in further friendships. Soon I was completely integrated into German life.

Nowadays, I generally feel more German than British but when England plays Germany at soccer, I realise that my conversion process has not yet been quite completed!

Expression to learn: *Ich liebe Deutschland!* (I love Germany!)

Avoid saying: You would have far more tourists if you still had a Royal Family!

2 ARRIVAL IN GERMANY

Most foreign visitors travel to Germany by plane. It is easy to spot the visitors arriving at the airports by the look of relief on their faces when they finally make it through passport and custom controls, having by then had their first experience of German officials. These are neither trained nor paid to be friendly, but simply to follow all the rules and regulations to the letter. The visitor is, of course, rather suspect from the moment his or her foot touches German soil, as Germans tend to be so busy complaining about life here, they can't imagine why anyone should want to come to the country for any lawful reason!

The visitor might be surprised to see so many non-German looking people waiting in the arrivals' hall. The explanation is that Germany has become very multicultural in recent years, particularly since Angela Merkel dispensed with border controls in 2015 at the height of the Syrian crisis.

If visitors take a taxi from the airport, they will find that most taxi drivers are foreigners, who don't know their way around or, like many of their German colleagues, prefer taking the scenic route in order to make more money, something common at airports all over the world!

Expressions to learn: *Ich hasse alle Beamte!* (I hate all officials!)

Avoid saying: I've never visited such a bureaucratic country!

It looks as if most of the Germans have left the country.

Was probably less divisive than copying Brexit!

3 REGISTRATION

People from Anglo-Saxon countries will be surprised to learn that if they stay in Germany for more than three months, they will have to register at the local authority where they live and obtain an Identity Card, which they must always carry with them when in public. However, this is not particularly German, as there are similar regulations in most other countries in continental Europe.

Apart from wishing to ensure that nobody stays in the country illegally, such registration is necessary to ensure that people pay income tax, since part of one's personal income tax goes to the local authority where one lives in order to finance some of its costs.

This registration system suffered a partial collapse during the Middle East refugee crisis of 2015, when hundreds of thousands of refugees and migrants entered Germany without going through any passport controls. In normal times, the registration system makes it difficult for people to disappear, but after the 2015 mass influx of people a terrible thing happened – the authorities no longer were in control, something that can give a German official extreme insomnia, or in extreme cases, a nervous breakdown!

Expressions to learn: *Das Meldewesen gib uns Sicherheit!* (The registration system gives us security!)

Avoid saying: Germans are control freaks!

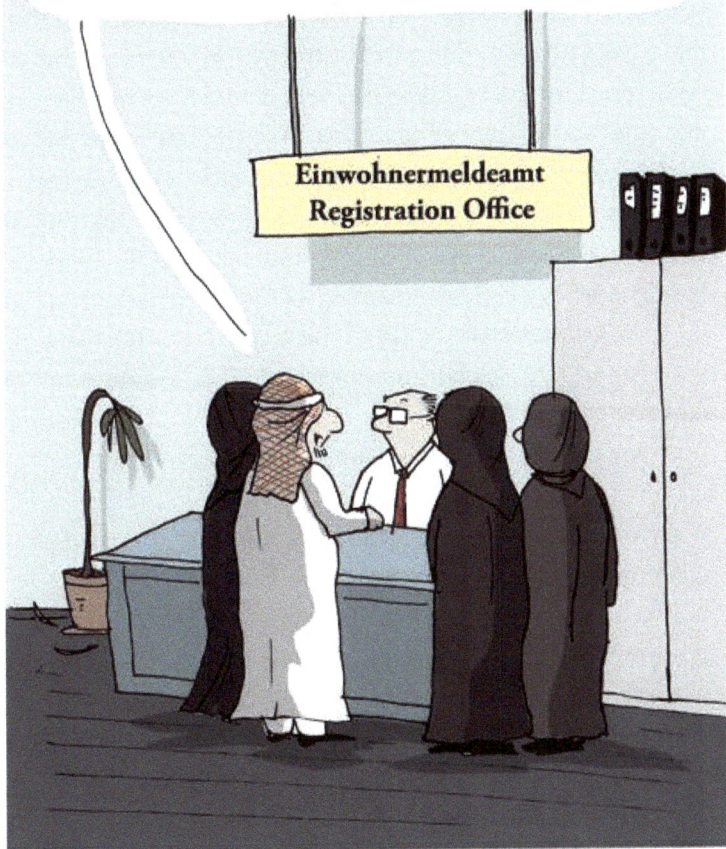

With so many foreigners in Germany, there is seldom a dull moment in the registration office.

4 BUREAUCRACY

Germany has thousands of regulations, without which the average German would feel very insecure. The visitor will be surprised at the number of things that need regulating if one really puts one's mind to it! Germany has invented laws and regulations for every possible aspect of life. For example, there are regulations concerning "peaceful periods" that set out exactly when one may make noise by such things as mowing the lawn, chopping wood, making loud music or shouting too loudly at the wife! Even shopping hours are strictly controlled. Foreigners have difficulty learning all these regulations but that isn't really a problem because there are many Germans who are expert at explaining them in the greatest if one contravenes some regulation or other. They then take much time and pleasure in demonstrating their knowledge!

However, the younger generation is not quite so expert as the older ones, probably because they have to spend such long hours in social media that they have no time to acquaint themselves with all the rules and regulations. Even the usual practice of shouting at perpetrators doesn't seem to work with the younger generation in many cases, no doubt because the loud music in the discos has made them half deaf! One wonders what the country will come to in a few years!

Expressions to learn: *Sei ruhig - es ist die offizielle Ruhezeit!* (Be quiet – it's the official quiet period!)

Avoid asking: Do you also have rules for making love?

Red is red, even if there is no traffic, but many youngsters seem to be colour blind.

5 THE TRUE KRAUT

As we shall see in the chapter on food, the nickname "Kraut" for German derives from the Germans' love of cabbage. Krauts are easily recognisable in the popular holiday resorts in southern Europe, as at about 6 am they will be seen placing a towel on one of the loungers around the hotel pool. This is, of course, forbidden in Germany!

When at home, the typical German is a very private person and rarely sees any reason for speaking to the neighbours unless, of course, they are in contravention of some regulation or other. Germans love to complain about the government, which, as in many other countries, was apparently elected by idiots.

Luckily, there are no rules and regulations for humour and despite their international reputation for being blessed with little humour, Krauts really enjoy a good joke from time to time. Contrary to the British, they don't like telling jokes against themselves and also have a problem seeing the funny side of cryptic jokes. However, the many comedy shows on Germany TV and the numerous side-splitting "sittings" at carnival time show how much Germans enjoy a good laugh. On New Year's Eve, no self-respecting Kraut would want to miss that old English short comedy film "Dinner for One", starring Freddie Frinton, something hardly known these days in the UK. But perhaps they like it so much because prior to the Brexit saga, most Germans were rather Anglophile.

Expressions to learn: *Wer hat diese Idioten gewählt?* (Who voted for these idiots?)

Avoid saying: So, you do have a sense of humour after all!

6 GOVERNMENT

At the insistence of the Western Allies, The Federal Republic of Germany, which was founded in 1949, has a strong federal system, although this was, and still is, highly uncommon in Western Europe. One might even suspect that the Allies thought this would help prevent Germany ever emerging once more as a strong economic force. If so, they completely underestimated the Germans!

The German parliament (*Bundestag*) is elected by proportional representation, elections taking place every four years. The second legislative chamber (*Bundesrat*) is made up of the representatives of the 16 federal states, which are also elected every four years but not at the same time as the *Bundestag* elections. New legislation is made difficult because the *Bundestag* and *Bundesrat* are often controlled by different political alliances. The federal system, also means that there are 16 different police forces, educational systems, building regulations and a thousand other things.

Angela Merkel has been German Chancellor since 2005 and although most Germans seem to complain constantly about the government, unlike babies, they nevertheless seem to dislike a change! By comparison with debates in the British House of Commons, debates in the German Bundestag are rather sleepy affairs (see cartoon!)

Expressions to learn: *Die Regierung ist dumm!* (The government is stupid!)

Avoid saying: With such electoral systems, it's a wonder that Germany isn't bankrupt!

Bundestag

House of Commons

16

7 OSSIES AND WESSIES

Communist rule came to an end in Eastern Europe in the late 1980's as a result of Gorbachev's policy of *perestroika* (modernisation) and in 1990, communist East Germany (originally the Soviet Zone of Germany) voted to join the Federal Republic of Germany. This took effect on 3 October of the same year.

The then Chancellor of West Germany, Helmut Kohl, promised the East Germans prosperity but severely underestimated the disastrous state of East Germany. East Germans equally underestimated how long it would take for them to have the same standard of living as West Germans. Most East German factories were uncompetitive, which soon resulted in mass closures, high unemployment and discontent.

Some West Germans still regard the East Germans (coined *Ossies*) as ungrateful for the huge amounts of money subsequently invested in the East Germany infrastructure, paid for by raising income and corporate taxes. At the same time, many East Germans are still bitterly disappointed about the high unemployment resulting from reunification and the supposed arrogance of West Germans (coined *Wessies*).

This illustrates well that it is never possible to please everybody the whole time and that sometimes even the best intentions are not enough. At the same time, it shows that one should be wary of trusting a politician!

Phrases to learn: *Demokratie ist eine feine Sache!* (Democracy is a fine thing!)

Avoid Saying: Democracy would be a fine thing if only it didn't need politicians!

8 THE GERMAN LANGUAGE

With his German translation of the Bible in 1534, Martin Luther started the standardisation of the German language. In the meantime, Germany has, of course, established a special committee to regulate German spelling and grammar!

The great advantage of this standardisation is something unbelievable by comparison to English - German is actually pronounced as it is written, although foreigners often have problems pronouncing certain vowels and consonants. Not wanting the language to have the reputation of being too simple, a grammar was invented that will make your head spin. For example, the definite article in English ("the") never changes, however used, which is rather boring, so things were made more interesting in German by having three different genders, which require three different definite articles, namely, *der, die* or *das*. As even that is reasonably simple, it was decided that both the nouns and the adjectives should change according to whether they are being used in the nominative, genitive, dative or accusative case. This clever invention resulted in 16 different versions of the definite article instead of just that boring old "the" in English!

Expression to learn: *Sprechen Sie Englisch?* (Do you speak English?)

Avoid saying: German grammar is horrible!

1. Open mouth wide.

2. Breathe in.

3. Breathe out while clearing your throat.

4. At the same time say: „Ich mache flache Sachen."

5. Clean the spectacles of your teacher.

9 THE METRIC SYSTEM

American and British visitors often have difficulty in adjusting to the metric system in Germany, which is, however, the global standard with the exception of the USA and Britain, these continuing to use the Imperial system of feet and inches, pounds etc. The metric system was invented by the French at the end of the 18th century and made mandatory by Napoleon in the German states he conquered in the early 19th century, when the French had the strongest army in Europe. Previously there had been numerous different regional measurement standards. Napoleon also introduced a metric clock, which divided the day into 10 hours of 100 minutes each, as well as a metric calendar, but even the French revolutionaries found these changes too radical and they were subsequently dropped.

If you drive to Germany from the UK with a British car, you may become so confused by driving on the right-hand side of the road instead of the left that you forget that the road signs are in kilometres and not miles. The speed limit in most built-up areas is 50 **kilometres** per hour and if you drive at 50 **miles** per hour by mistake, you will be exceeding the speed limit by a massive 30 kilometres per hour. If not caught on the spot, you will later receive a souvenir of your visit comprising a high-quality photograph of yourself as driver and a hefty fine. However, you will not lose your driving licence, as would happen to a German.

Phrases to learn: *Das Zwölfersystem muss verboten werden!* (The Imperial system must be forbidden).

Avoid saying: The metric system was obviously invented by poor mathematicians unable to multiply or divide by 12!

10 THE ENVIRONMENT (1)

Most Germans are keen on protecting the environment. Growing fears of global warming resulted in the ecology party (the "Greens") achieving second place in Germany in the 2019 European Election, receiving 20.5% of the votes. The Greens' influence on politics in recent years has led to the government taking measures some time ago to close all nuclear power stations by 2022. Ironically, the shortfall in electricity is being made up in the meantime by importing it from Poland (78 % coal-based) and France (62% nuclear- based). This situation may continue for some time, since environmentalists are blocking the construction of the new power lines necessary to distribute power from the new wind and solar parks in Germany, which is surely ironic!

The government would like most diesel- and petrol-powered vehicles replaced by electrically-powered ones as soon as possible, although nobody knows from where the additional electricity will come in the short-term or whether the German car industry will survive this sudden change in policy. Electrically-powered vehicles are simpler to build than those with internal combustion engines, meaning that fewer production workers will be needed. The Greens are certain that all those who lose jobs in the car industry will find new ones in environmentally- friendly industries. Whether this is realistic or not seems to be secondary to the satisfying feeling that Germany is doing something to reduce harmful emissions and that the Swedish activist, Greta, will be pleased that her work is not in vain!

Expressions to learn: *E-Autos sind geil!* (Electric cars are sexy!)

Avoid saying: I don't believe global warming is caused by humans!

11 THE ENVIRONMENT (2)

Another important factor in protecting the environment is recycling household waste, of which Germans produce an average of some 220 kg per person per year, almost one third more than the EU average! There is, of course, a law concerning the disposal of household waste but the detailed regulations vary slightly from one administrative area to another. However, all household waste must be divided into four categories - paper, plastic, biological waste and general waste and disposed of in four different rubbish bins distinguished by colours. In addition, each local authority has a central refuse disposal centre for both normal and special waste, such as electrical equipment.

The strict rules for rubbish disposal are very positive psychologically, as people have the feeling that they are improving the environment. This helps considerably in cancelling out bad consciences for consuming so much meat, driving SUVs and indulging in such other environmental killers as air flights and holidays on cruise ships! A further improvement might be for waste collection centres to be located in remote locations, so that people don't see the tons of harmful waste they produce - otherwise, they might suffer insomnia or a nervous breakdown instead of enjoying life!

Expressions to learn: *Trennmüll rettet die Welt!* (Rubbish separation saves the world!)

Avoid saying: It would surely be simpler and cheaper to export all that waste to Africa!

12 CARS

German men seem to have a difficult time deciding which to love more, their wives or their cars, but in many cases one has the impression that the cars have won this battle. Perhaps this is only logical because cars not only usually do what they are told but it is easier and cheaper to trade in an old car for a new one than it is doing the same with a wife!

It is probably also only logical that cars seem to play a special role in German life, since the motorcar was invented in Germany by Carl Benz in 1885 and German car production currently ranks third globally after China and Japan.

The first *Autobahn* (motorways / highways) were built in Germany in the 1930s and the network has been extensively extended since the Second World War, some 70% of the *autobahn* having no speed limit. However, having no speed limits hardly makes journeys quicker because of the constant increase in both the numbers of German vehicles on the roads and the amount of international traffic passing through Germany. This all peaks in the summer due to the school holidays in Germany, as well as the many northern Europeans who travel to holiday resorts in southern Europe via Germany. Despite the numerous *Autobahn*, Germany then often becomes gridlocked.

Expressions to learn: *Ich liebe mein Auto!* (I love my car!)

Avoid saying: Cars are a major source of global warming.

13 PUBLIC TRANSPORT

Not only the country's road system had to be rebuilt following the Second World War but also the railway lines. Today, the country has an excellent rail network, with the ultra-fast Inter City Expresses (*ICE's*) and the Intercity trains (*IC's*) providing a fast and comfortable service between the larger towns and cities, the metropolitan areas being served by a combination of underground trains (*U-Bahn*) and a suburban train service (*S-Bahn*).

In the large towns and cities there is usually a good local bus service but until recently, long-distance bus services were banned because the government wanted to protect the state-owned railways from cheap competition.

In the 1980`s, one could still set one's watch by the punctuality of train arrivals and departures. However, a lack of investment in the railways has sadly led to a serious deterioration in service and many delays. Today, one needs not only a reliable watch but also a mobile phone to check the many delays and cancellations. If you wish to relive the 1980's train experience in Germany, you must go to Switzerland, where everything still works like clockwork, although this has nothing to do with the fact that the Swiss dominate watchmaking!

Phrases to learn: W*ieviel Verspätung hat mein Zug?* (How late is my train?)

Avoid saying: Why is everything going downhill in Germany?

14 BUILDING

To comply with the building regulations, one has to build to high standards, which makes building in Germany expensive by comparison to most other countries. In addition, the fact that each of the 16 federal states has its own building regulations prevents cost-saving through standardisation. The cost of complying with the high insulation standards necessary to comply with the energy policy is also a factor.

When planning projects, German architects seem to place most emphasis on the external appearance of a building, rather than ensuring that it functions well. Architects also take little interest in what buildings cost – unless the building owner employs a cost planner (which is unusual), he or she will often only find out the true cost when the building is completed! Buildings built by state institutions are notorious for being completed far too late and with enormous cost-overruns. This rarely leads to any consequences for the officials concerned – it must be comforting for them to know that the tax-payer will foot the bill anyway!

The fact that the quality of the workmanship in new buildings is so high must have something to do with German air because in recent years many young Germans seem to have developed an aversion to physical work and the resultant shortage of skilled building workers has only been resolved by employing foreigners. After only a short time, they begin to work to the same high standards as Germans as a result of breathing German air!

Phrases to learn: *Deutsche Bauqualität ist fantastisch!* (German building quality is fantastic!)

Avoid asking: How many building owners commit suicide when they find out the final cost of their house?

15 HOMES

Not only the high building standards drive up costs but also the lack of building land. There is great opposition for ecological reasons to zoning new building land, most people not realising that only about 15% of the country is covered by buildings, roads, railways etc. High building and land costs mean that the majority of Germans can't afford to own a house or flat / condominium and Germany has the second lowest home-ownership rate of all developed countries (only 46.5% by comparison with 63,5% in the UK, 64,5% in the USA, 77% % in Spain and a massive 96,4 % in Romania!). As houses in particular are extremely expensive to buy or rent, 57% of Germans live in flats (only 19% in the UK).

The fact that there are regulations for everything is, of course, a great advantage for flat-dwellers, as it prevents people being too egoistic in their lifestyles. Thus, every block of flats has "house rules" that regulate everything from making undue noise to the use of balconies. If there is no caretaker, the occupiers have responsibility for cleaning the staircases and entrance halls on a weekly rota basis that helps them keep fit! When renting a flat, it is not unusual to find the landlord has not fitted out the kitchen, the tenant being expected to do this. Where this is the case, when people move, they often take their kitchens with them! Many flat-dwellers miss having a garden, which is the reason for the many well-maintained allotment gardens near the larger cities. One could easily have the impression that even in their spare time, Germans like to work!

Expressions to learn: *Es ist verboten Wäsche auf dem Balkon auszuhängen!* (It's forbidden hang out washing on the balcony!)

Avoid saying: I couldn't care less about all those stupid house rules!

Why are they throwing those nice kitchen cabinets away?

They aren't - they're just moving to a new flat.

Not all rented flats have fitted kitchens but at least they have fitted bathrooms and toilets!

16 BATHROOMS

Bathrooms in Germany don't differ much from those in the rest of western Europe. However, in older properties one may encounter a rather strange-looking toilet with a round outlet at the front, the rest comprising a shallow basin with little water in it. This is the *Flachtoilette* ("flat toilet"). Germans are very health-conscious and the original reason for this strange contraption was that it made it easier to collect samples for analysis by the doctor, or simply to check oneself that everything looked healthy (ugh!!).

One will also often encounter a sign on the wall behind the toilet with the request: *Bitte nicht im Stehen pinkeln!* ("please don't pee whilst standing!"), which presumably only applies to males. However, men will be relieved to learn that in a court case in 2015, it was ruled that men may indeed urinate while standing, despite many women not wanting to stand for this nonsense any longer!

In private homes, one is expected to use the squeegee to clean the shower or bath after use, which in the case of the shower is really only possible if one does so immediately after use and is, therefore, naked. Adult Germans shower on average 4.5 times a week and, assuming the shower cleaning takes about five minutes, one arrives at the conclusion that Germans work naked for an average of almost 20 hours per year. However, this doesn't worry them too much, as Germans seem to love visiting the nudist beaches in summer and can dream that they are on holiday whilst doing the cleaning!

Phrases to Learn: *Ich liebe es die Dusche zu putzen!* (I love cleaning the shower!)

Questions to avoid: Do men really have to clean the shower too?

Bitte nicht im
Stehen pinkeln!

Don't pee
while standing!

There are simpler ways!

17 FOOD

As already mentioned, the nickname "Kraut" comes from the supposed love of cabbage. *Sauerkraut* ("sour cabbage") is very popular and is made of white cabbage. It has a sour taste because it has been sliced and preserved in salt. It may be an acquired taste but it is very healthy. The famous British explorer, Captain Cook, knew this and insisted that his sailors ate it during long voyages in the 18th century in order to prevent scurvy. This resulted in the illness being known in German as the "English sickness". Although pickled red cabbage is popular in many countries, Germans prefer to slice and cook it. It appeals to most tastes and is a good accompaniment to game or fatty dishes.

Although Germany is sometimes nicknamed *Krautland*, a better name might be *Wurstland* ("Sausage Land"), as Germans love sausage and produce more than 1,500 different varieties, either for heating in water or grilling. The most interesting one is probably the Bavarian white sausage (*Weißwurst*), made of veal and covered in a transparent skin, which causes most foreigners to think it looks similar to a condom! Despite a love-hate relationship with the Turkish population in Germany, one of the most popular snacks is the Turkish *Döner*, which is made of slices of meat with seasoning in a bread roll.

Germany only has a small coastline and most of the country is far from the sea, so before refrigeration, saltwater fish wasn't widely eaten and fish and chips is only known as a joke about British cuisine!

Expressions to learn: *Bratwurst mit Pommes, bitte!* (A grilled sausage with chips, please!)

Avoid saying: That white sausage looks disgusting.

The Germans don't think much of British cuisine!

18 TEA AND COFFEE

Before coffee and tea arrived in Europe in the 17th century, people usually drank warm beer with their breakfast. Today it is coffee or tea. Germans drink almost twice as much coffee as tea and only in East Frisia on the North Sea coast, where the first German tea merchants were based, will you get a nice "cuppa!". Unfortunately, the East Frisians spoil their tea by drinking it without milk and with candied sugar. Elsewhere in Germany, you are well advised to switch to drinking coffee, as you will otherwise probably be served a glass of hot (but not boiling) water, with a teabag and slice of lemon in the saucer. Even to get this, you will have to ask for "black" tea, since many Germans only drink tea when they are feeling ill, making it out of anything from fruit to plant leaves (ugh!)

The good news is that German coffee is usually very good. Traditionally it was made by pouring boiling water over a filter filled with ground coffee but these days Italian-style coffee is very popular, many homes having their own coffee machines. Traditional afternoon coffee with some delicious German cake is a must, my favourite being a Black Forest cherry gateau, which is baked with a generous portion of cherry schnapps. However, more than one slice may put your driving licence at risk!

Expressions to learn: *Eine Kanne Schwarztee, bitte, mit drei Beuteln.* (A pot of black tea please with three teabags!)

Avoid saying: This tea looks like washing-up water.

19 BEER

Although Germans may have no idea how to make a good cup of tea, they are world champions in respect of beer, the country having more than 1,500 breweries and producing a mind-boggling 5,000 varieties. Most of these are only produced and consumed in a particular region and some are even only brewed according to the season. German beer is, of course, produced in accordance with some regulations, namely the *Reinheitsgebot* ("Purity Regulation ") of 1516, which says that beer must only contain hops, malt and water. Unfortunately, the EU has ruled that beer containing other ingredients must also be allowed to be sold in Germany, but most Germans prefer their own pure variety and complain about the EU's interference in such an important matter.

The most popular type of beer is the Pils, which it is said should take exactly seven minutes to pour, in order to ensure that it has a good "head" of foam on the top. This can only be achieved by rather slow pouring, so if you are particularly thirsty, immediately order two Pils!

Traditional German "folk music" is commonly played in the many beer gardens in summer, and in the beer halls in winter. This usually creates a relaxed atmosphere, with most people joining in the singing of well-known songs, whilst linking arms and swaying to and fro in time to the waltzes.

For those struggling to speak German, it all becomes much easier after a few glasses of beer!

Expressions to learn: *Noch ein Bier, bitte!* (Another beer please!)

Avoid saying: The music is so boring!

German beer improves your German

1st glass	-	No change.
2nd glass	-	You don't feel shy speaking German.
3nd glass	-	German friends seem to understand what you are saying.
4th glass	-	You give up on German grammar.
5th glass	-	You start to mix up German and English.
6th glass	-	You try out some German swear words.
7th glass	-	You start to speak Bavarian German.
8th glass	-	You give up trying to speak at all and fall asleep.

20 OTHER DRINKS

In the summer, many Germans like to add some mineral water to their wine, apple juice etc. to make it more refreshing. When mixed with mineral water, it is called a *Schorle*, the word probably originating from the old South-West German dialect for *sprudeln* ("sparkling ").

As already mentioned, Germans are very health-conscious and although tap water throughout Germany is very healthy, many prefer to drink bottled mineral water instead. However, most men seem to be also sceptical about the quality of the mineral water and prefer beer, wine or schnapps!

Apple juice (*Apfelsaft*) is very popular throughout Germany and when starting to ferment to produce a form of cider (*Most*) is a refreshing drink called *Süßmost*. In the area around Frankfurt am Main, a local form of cider, known as *Apfelwein* ("apple wine") is very popular. It is traditionally accompanied by hard cheese with onions and vinegar, known in German as *Handkäs mit Musik* ("hand cheese with music"), the onions being the reason for the music! At the traditional Christmas fairs in the Frankfurt area, the apple wine is spiced and served hot. Elsewhere, spiced hot wine (*Glühwein*) is the usual outside hot drink in winter and is very popular when skiing. From personal experience, I must warn that it is not wise to stop off at one of the bars on the ski slopes and drink more than two glasses of *Glühwein* if one is afterwards intending to ski down the rest of the mountain!

Phrases to learn: *Ich finde Apfesaftlschorle himmlisch im Sommer!* (I think that apple juice with mineral water is heavenly in summer!)

Avoid saying: I wouldn't dream of spoiling my wine by putting water in it!

21 STAMMTISCH

Most German pubs have a table displaying a small notice *"Stammtisch"*, meaning *Regulars' Table*. This is an important part of German culture: in most small towns and villages, this is not only where the locals meet for a drink but is also a social meeting point, where politics, soccer etc. can be discussed heatedly, but usually without loss of life! Typical German card games are also played there but Brits will probably miss the darts' board found in almost all British pubs. However, perhaps this is a good thing, since the heated *Stammtisch* discussions might otherwise sometimes result in the darts being used to drive home a point!

The *Stammtisch* was originally exclusively for men but the relentless march of women's rights reached the German pub some time ago and one of the few refuges now left for men is the men's toilets. This means that the constant visits to the loo by the men aren't necessarily because they have consumed so much beer but because of the need for a short break from the female gossip. Some women also need loo breaks to escape the men's endless talk about politics, soccer and cars. Perhaps the solution would be to have segregated *Stammtische* for men and women!

Expressions to learn: *Wer bezahlt die nächste Runde?* (Who is paying the next round?)

Avoid saying: Beer encourages people to speak a lot of nonsense!

46

22 RESTAURANTS AND PUBS

You won't find many German-style restaurants in other countries and the number of truly German restaurants in Germany seems to be declining. As we shall see later, Germans are great travellers and at home like to eat some of the food they have experienced abroad.

In addition to eating in restaurants and hotels, one can also eat well in the many smaller *Gasthäuser* ("guesthouses") and German-style pubs. The Bavarian particularly likes to eat and drink in a beer hall or beer garden, where he can get his teeth into traditional food, such as a huge pork chop, and has little interest Italian food, as the pasta might ruin his beautiful traditional shirt.

German restaurants usually have speciality menus for certain seasonal food, such as game (wild boar, venison etc.) in the autumn and early winter. White asparagus is a great favourite from mid-April until 24th June – this is not a regulation but is based on the tradition that "once the cherries are red, asparagus is dead!" Generally, Germans tend to eat large portions but many restaurants offer smaller "pensioner" portions.

Both beer and wine are popular accompaniments to meals. The white and rosé wines are excellent but I feel that one must have been born in Germany to like the red variety! As far as beer is concerned, the measure mark on the glass is well below the top, so even with a generous "head" on the beer, you are not being cheated!

Expressions to learn: *Eine kleine Portion, bitte.* (A small portion, please.)

Avoid saying: I miss my Yorkshire pudding!

23 SHOPPING

In the USA there are many derelict town centres, caused by retailers and businesses moving to green field locations. In Germany, restrictions on zoning building land in such locations have prevented something similar happening. However, the number of vacant shops in German city centres is now growing slowly as a result of competition from internet retailers, so Germany may also be heading for deserted town centres in a few years!

Visitors from Anglo-Saxon countries will be surprised to learn that the trading hours for retailers are strictly regulated by the local authority and vary slightly from one place to another. Sunday trading is generally only permitted about four times a year. However, bakers, pharmacies and filling stations may trade on Sundays, as well as retail outlets at railway stations and airports.

When shopping, please remember that shop staff are generally overworked and underpaid, as well as having frayed nerves and very fragile constitutions! The only joy they seem to get out of work is at the tills of supermarkets and large stores, when they love to put the customers under pressure to pack away their purchases at the speed of light to make room for the next customer!

Phrases to learn: *Wo ist der nächste Bäcker, bitte?* (Where is the next baker please?)

Avoid asking: Do you realise it is really the customer who pays your wages?

24 QUEUEING

Although there are rules and regulations for just about everything, there is one glaring gap, namely queueing. This is something of a shock for visiting Brits, who simply love to queue wherever they can. The author of humorous books about Britain, George Mikes, once wrote that if one plants a bus stop anywhere in Britain, a queue will form automatically within a few minutes! This is definitely not the case in Germany – there, when a bus arrives at a bus stop, boarding becomes a matter of the survival of the fittest. As an ex-rugby player, it reminds me of playing in the scrum!

At government offices, one is in a different world. When one enters the office, one usually has to pull a number out of a small machine and then wait patiently until one's number is called. If the office closes for lunch, the number is cancelled and after the lunch break, one might easily be at the back of the queue once more. Rules are rules and complaining doesn't help!

In large stores there is at least some orderly queuing at the tills because of the railing between the tills. However, when things are busy and another till suddenly opens, take care not to be killed in the rush!

Expressions to learn: *Wo kann ich Schlange stehen üben?* (Where can I practice standing in a queue?)

Avoid saying: Seeing Germans fighting to get on a bus or train makes one wonder why rugby or American football aren't more popular in this country!

Queuing in Germany

Queuing in Britain

25 PUNCTUALITY

In Germany, punctuality seems to be even more important than holiness! At university, it used to be a tradition that both lecturers and students could arrive 15 minutes late for lectures, this leeway being known as the "academic quarter". It used to apply to all appointments but in business today one is expected to be punctual, being late for a meeting being regarded as disrespectful.

However, arriving a day too early for a meeting is also to be avoided. This happened to me on one occasion, when my secretary made an appointment for me in Munich and, by mistake, entered it my diary and booked my flight from Berlin for a day too early. When I arrived at the reception desk of the firm I was visiting, I was told that I was more than over-punctual! Recovering from the shock, I decided that it was not worth flying back to Berlin, so I took an unexpected day off work and visited a number of interesting museums I would otherwise never have seen! I enjoyed this unforeseen relaxation so much that I decided not to fire my secretary after all!

The fetish for punctuality does not seem to apply to some women in private life but I suppose it is time-consuming trying on at least four different outfits before finally finding the right one!

Expressions to learn: *Ich muss pünktlich sein!* (I must be punctual!)

Avoid saying: Germans can sometimes be so small-minded!

It's scenes like this that prove that men are from Mars and women are from Venus.

26 CELEBRATING

It is commonly thought that Germans can't let their hair down and celebrate but this is completely wrong. For example, carnival is celebrated madly in some parts of the country in the six days prior to Ash Wednesday. Another popular celebration is the *Oktoberfest* in Munich, which starts in the last September week in order to confuse foreigners! It is celebrated on the *Theresienwiese*, which is a pasture that is developed temporally with a fair ground and huge marquees housing beer halls. Here, the beer flows freely while a band plays traditional music and songs. The *Oktoberfest* is today so famous that the visitors come from all over the world but mostly dress in typical Bavarian style The *Oktoberfest* has now become so popular that copies have emerged all over Germany and also in other countries.

Birthdays are often celebrated in style, particularly "round ones" (30, 40, 50 etc.). A double number in a birthday (i.e. 44, 55, 66 etc.) are so-called "Schnapps years" that also call for special celebration, as do, of course, important wedding anniversaries. You will then learn how musical and poetic many Germans are, as they often compose special songs for these occasions, as well as poems about the people at the centre of the celebrations. Despite the difficult German grammar mentioned earlier, there seem to be far more words in German that rhyme than in English and, of course, when making up poems, one doesn't anyway have to follow the correct word order quite so slavishly – Germans can be very flexible after all!

Songs not to learn: "Happy Birthday". (It's always sung in English and is pronounced "Happy Birsday"!)

Avoid saying: Unbelievable – and I previously thought Germans didn't know how to celebrate!

27 FATHERS' DAY

Father's Day is celebrated in Germany on Ascension Day, which is 39 days after Easter Sunday and is a public holiday. Whoever planned Fathers' Day ensured that it is always falls on a Thursday, which means that by taking the Friday off work, the fathers can enjoy themselves to the full, as they have a long weekend to recover from the excesses!

To make up for the stress of having children, fathers are allowed to let down their hair on this day, when many go for a hike with their friends, often pulling a cartload of beer behind them - hiking and singing all those old songs at the same time makes one very thirsty! As the day proceeds, ever more inhibitions are thrown off and the fathers end up behaving in such a way that they would never tolerate from their children. However, tradition says that fathers are allowed to do such outrageous things once a year. Nevertheless, their spouses will probably give them a hard time when they finally return home, although it will fall on deaf ears, since by then the husbands will be immune to any criticism and have that long weekend to recover from making the most of this wonderful yearly event.

Expressions to learn: *Echtes Vaterglück kommt nur einmal im Jahr!* (The real joy of fatherhood only comes once a year!)

Avoid saying: What a terrible role-model they are for their children!

On father's day, fathers re-live the happy, wild times before they had children!

Father's Day in Germany is a public holiday when men go off hiking with their best friends and plenty of beer.

28 WEDDINGS (1)

The Anglo-Saxon tradition of the bridegroom holding a "stag night" and the bride a "hen party" shortly before the wedding has spread to Germany, but usually only for the first marriage! Church marriages in Germany are not recognised by the state and if one wants to have a church wedding, it is usual practice to marry first at a local authority registry office. This is just a small affair for the immediate family and a couple of really close friends. The church wedding is then the main event and usually takes place the day after the registry office wedding. As some 33% of German marriages end in divorce today, it would perhaps be wiser only to have church marriage, since then one wouldn't have to go to court to get an expensive divorce one day!

It is an old tradition that on the evening before the wedding, a celebration known as a *Polterabend* is held at the bride's house, when all types of old porcelain and crockery, including the odd old toilet and washbasin, are thrown on the ground to make a loud noise to detract the evil spirits and bring luck to the marriage. The word *Polter* means "clatter" and has the same root as the word *poltergeist*.

At a traditional German church wedding, the bride and groom enter the church together, not as in most English-speaking countries, where the bride enters the on the arm of her father, who "gives his daughter away". The German version is definitely more logical because most young women today wouldn't regard themselves as belonging to their father and being capable of being "given away"!

Expressions to learn: *Darf ich meine alte Toilette in Deinen Garten schmeißen?* (Can throw my old toilet in your garden?)

Avoid asking: Why is it not forbidden to make so much noise smashing those old things?

29 WEDDINGS (2)

It is a tradition that the bride and groom open the dancing at the wedding reception by dancing a Viennese waltz. As most Germans know nothing of ballroom dancing, they usually start taking dancing lessons a few weeks before the wedding and are truly thankful when they complete their waltz on the "big day" without tripping over!

It is also a tradition that the bride is "captured" by wedding guests during the reception, while the bridegroom is distracted. The bride is usually taken to a nearby pub, where the customers can enjoy free drinks until the bridegroom finally finds his bride and can claim her once more by paying for the drinks as a form of ransom money.

When my wife and I married, my wife persuaded her friends not to kidnap her because I didn't know the area around my wife's home very well and had told her that I would not waste valuable drinking time by trying to find her!

Although it used to be a tradition that the bride's parents paid for the wedding reception, this seems to have gone out of fashion, no doubt to the relief of parents with two or more daughters!

Phrases to learn: *Die Braut sieht so schön aus!* (The bride looks so beautiful!)

Avoid saying: He must have proposed to her when he was drunk!

Many German men are fanatical football fans.

30 CHRISTMAS

In recent years, Christmas seems to have developed from a religious celebration to a retailers' festival. In Germany, virtually every town and village has a Christmas market, which seems to start earlier every year. Today, there is an American-style Father Christmas in most large stores, although he was unknown in Germany until a few years' ago. Instead, Germany has always had a St Nicholas, who visits children on St Nicholas Day (6th December). In some parts of Germany, he brings his horrible-looking assistant, Ruprecht, with him, whose role is to punish children, who have misbehaved in the previous months. In practice, he never has to punish anybody but it certainly helps keep the children under control, while St Nicholas gives the children small presents in return for them reciting a short poem or singing a Christmas Carol.

Both children and adults receive their Christmas presents on the evening of Christmas Eve. They are mysteriously deposited under the traditional Christmas tree in the lounge by the *Christkind* (an angel-like being that nobody has ever seen), the children being distracted elsewhere. By the time they return to the lounge, the *Christkind* has already disappeared once more. Some children think it is all arranged by Amazon!

Phrases to learn: *Was ein schöner Weihnachtsbaum.* (What a beautiful Christmas tree!)

Avoid asking: Why can't I have my presents on Christmas Day like the rest of the world?

31 PARTIES

Germans seem to love partying and don't need some special event to have one. In addition to parties for birthdays, wedding anniversaries etc., you might find yourself invited to a party in connection with the final of the soccer world cup, somebody moving into a new home, etc.

If you are invited to a party, you must be careful not to arrive early but also not more than about 15 minutes late. You will be expected to bring a small present with you, the usual ones being a bouquet of flowers for the hostess and a bottle of wine for the host. Even if you know your hosts very well and are on very familiar terms with them, you must still follow some old-fashioned rules in greeting them. The men must always greet the ladies first and should do this by holding them gently, while giving them a gentle "peck" on each cheek. The ladies greet each other in a similar way and the men shake hands with each other. Kissing on the lips is only for lovers!

The English song "Happy Birthday" is sung at most birthday parties in Germany but take care to pronounce it correctly as "Happy Birsday"! Unfortunately, Germans don't know the "Hokey Cokie" song and dance, which is fun when all join in. My wife and I have done our best to introduce it into Germany to lighten up parties, which might be the reason why haven't been invited to many recently!

Phrases to learn, but only if you don't blush too easily: *Du siehst überhaupt nicht wie 50 aus!* (You don't look anything like 50!)

Avoid saying: All those poems are so boring!

How to greet your hostess at a party

Wrong approach!!

Right approach!

32 TRAVEL

When one visits southern Europe in summer, one can easily have the impression that it is full of Germans. However, in 2018 the most popular holiday destination for Germans was their own country, where some 34% also spent their main holiday. However, as employees usually have six week's holiday a year, many Germans travel somewhere on holiday at least twice a year. Thus, although the population of Germany is only 83 million, some 80 million Germans went abroad on holiday in 2018, the most popular destinations being Spain (10%), Italy (9.5%) and Austria (8.1%).

Just like the British and Scandinavians, the Germans seem to like to congregate together in the most popular holiday destinations, so if you visit Spain, you will find one resort favoured by the Germans, the next one by the Brits and another one by the Scandinavians. Of course, some resorts are mixed and where this is the case, the Brits always accuse the Krauts of reserving loungers around the swimming pools at the crack of dawn and vice versa!

It seems strange that some Germans love their schnitzel and sauerkraut when on holiday, despite the great choice of local dishes. However, some Brits aren't much better and even in Spain some still expect their British-style fish and chips!

Phrases to learn: *Es ist verboten die Liegen zu reservieren!* (It's forbidden to reserve the loungers!)

Avoid saying: I wonder if they also behave so badly at home?

Typical - at 7am you Krauts have already reserved all the loungers!

We are hard workers, used to getting up early in the morning, not like you lazy Brits!

33 LEISURE

In the past, most Germans were members of one or more local clubs or organisations, such as soccer, tennis, gymnastic, hiking, cycling or skiing clubs, the music, choir or carnival association, or the voluntary Fire Brigade, Red Cross etc. Unfortunately, it seems that the main meeting place for many of the younger generation is now the internet. As a result, in many places club life is slowly dying or the membership numbers falling year by year.

However, cycling is an exception and has increased greatly in popularity in recent years, partly due to the invention of electric bikes, which are particularly in fashion with the older generation. Unfortunately, many of these are not used to cycling at speeds up to 25 km per hour and if you spot one of these seniors heading in your direction, take cover! Hiking is also still very popular and presents virtually no danger of being injured by a member of the older generation! But beware – my impression is that German hikers are much fitter than the Brits, so have a good excuse if you are not feeling up to a 30 kilometer hike!

As in most countries, Germans also spend much of their leisure time watching television. The majority of peak-viewing seems to be taken up with quizzes, talent shows and detective series, the most popular detective series being *Tatort* ("crime scene"), shown on Sunday evenings. At the rate that people are murdered on television, it's surprising that there are any Germans left!

Expressions to learn: *Ich liebe Tatort.* (I love Tatort.)

Avoid saying: Hiking is too tiring and boring for me!

70

34 SPORT

Germany is a very sporting nation that has either won world or European championships in a wide range of sports, such as soccer, handball, field hockey, volleyball, basketball, tennis, ice hockey and cycling, as well as in all types of winter sport. However, the most popular sport is soccer, which is played by more than 14 million Germans over the age of 14.

Whereas the British attitude to sport is that it is better to have played and lost than not to have played at all, Germans seem only to play games that they think they can win. Although cricket and rugby were played widely in Germany in the late 19th century, Germans soon concentrated on other sports in which they had a better chance of success.

The top German professional soccer league, the Bundesliga, has become rather boring in recent years because it has been dominated by Bayern Munich. The main reason for this is a string of championship wins going back to the 1980s. As result of all these years of success, Bayern is now by far the richest club in Germany and can usually outbid all other German clubs for the best players. Accordingly, most German soccer fans now either love or hate Bayern. There seems little chance that the situation will change in the near future because financial investors are not allowed to own or control German football clubs. This seems an outdated attitude because money now seems to rule almost all sports except tiddlywinks!

Expressions to learn: *Ich hasse Bayern München!* (I hate Bayern Munich!)

Avoid asking: Why must Germans always play to win?

The Germans are becoming more and more anglophile!

35 CLUBS

As mentioned, there are a huge number of clubs in Germany, despite the fact that at one time they were largely forbidden. The reason for this was that following the French Revolution in 1789, the authorities in the German states were very nervous that such ideas might spread to their areas and endanger their privileged positions. Laws were introduced forbidding gatherings that were not in connection with organisations that had been formed and registered in accordance with restrictive new laws. Lenin had apparently heard of this, as he once said that trust is good but control is better!

There are no longer such strict restrictions on the purposes of clubs and it is no problem, for example, to form political parties, provided that they are in accordance with the German constitution. Nevertheless, virtually all organisations that are not in a corporate form are in the form of a registered association and have a constitution, management board etc. Otherwise every member would be responsible for the debts of the club and could be sued if the club caused somebody financial loss. This applies even to such organisations as allotment garden associations. It is, therefore, no wonder that there are about 630,000 registered associations in Germany. If one looked at the register of clubs, one would be amazed by the great variety. In fact, registered clubs of all sorts are so widespread in Germany that it is said that when more than three people meet together, they automatically form one!

Expressions to learn: *Wir müssen unbedingt einen Club gründen!* (We really must form a club!)

Avoid saying: All this bureaucracy would drive me crazy!

36 HEALTH

Germany has an excellent health system, which requires all employees to have health insurance, 50% of the costs being paid by the employer. If one wants better cover, such as being treated by the head surgeon or having a single room in hospital, one can opt out of the state system and have private insurance instead. However, private insurance is very expensive.

The fact that the basic health insurance provides very good cover leads to people being very health-conscious and consulting their doctor for every little ache and pain. If one feels ill, one can take up to three days "sick leave" from work on full pay without the need for a doctor's certificate. Doctors are often pressurised by patients to certify them a sick for longer than three days, even if they are not really ill. The doctor will then often certify that the patient has a "circulation disorder", (i.e. the blood circulation is not functioning properly), an illness that seems largely unknown outside Germany!

Doctors' waiting rooms always seem to be full, not necessarily because so many people are ill, but because many widows and widowers feel lonely and enjoy a free chat with their GP!

Take care never to become ill on a Wednesday afternoon, as almost all doctors' surgeries are then closed!

Expressions to learn: *Ich habe eine Kreislaufstörung.* (I am suffering from a circulation disorder.)

Avoid saying: I have never heard of such an illness!

37 SEX

The famous author of humorous books about the British, George Mikes, once wrote that, whereas the continentals have sex, the British have a hot water bottle! The Germans couldn't be more different and are much more open about sex than Anglo-Saxons. In summer, at the first glimpse of sun, they flock to the many nudist beaches and don't think twice about going to the mixed sauna, where it is forbidden to wear anything! I once experienced the amusing sight of an American being thrown out of the mixed sauna in a German hotel because he refused to take off his bathing trunks. When a member of the hotel staff told him that it was unhygienic to wear the trunks, he replied in a huff that it was against the rules of decency for naked males and females to mix in the sauna!

The relaxed attitude to nakedness and sex in Germany was helped by a female ex-Second World War pilot, Beate Uhse, who seems to have discovered that sex is almost as good as flying, because she opened a chain of sex shops in the 1950s, which did so well that it was subsequently floated on the German stock exchange. It was the first time that Germans found being a shareholder could be sexy!

I am slightly disappointed that I have not yet any detailed rules and regulations about sex, so I can only recommend learning by doing!

Expressions to learn: *Ich hasse Wärmflaschen*! (I hate hot water bottles!)

Avoid saying: I've never seen a pair of boobs like that before!

Quite contrary to the Brits and Yanks, Germans have no problem in running around naked!

38 TAXATION

The German taxation system is extremely complicated, since the authorities wish to ensure that nobody is able to find a way of minimising their tax liability. In fact, there is said to be more literature in respect of German taxation than in respect of all other taxation systems in the world put together! However, the complicated system is also a result of lobbyists, who protect their clientele's interests so well that there are hundreds of special tax rules to the benefit of certain groups. This is, of course, excellent for tax advisers, who can save their clients a fortune by knowing all the tricks available and make good money for themselves at the same time. The fact that today there are some 98,000 tax advisers in Germany, some 66% more than 20 years' ago, speaks for itself!

Despite the government's extreme efforts to prevent tax evasion, firms operating globally can usually find easy ways of paying virtually no tax in Germany by using official EU tax havens, such as Ireland. Such legal ways of lowering the tax burden are not available to private individuals, so for years, many of the wealthiest Germans avoided tax illegally by diverting part of their income to "black" bank accounts in Switzerland, which was once one of the best tax havens in the world. In the meantime, this is too dangerous because so many employees of Swiss banks have made money by selling information on "black accounts" to the German tax authorities. These days it seems almost dangerous to make an innocent trip to Switzerland, in case one is suspected of being involved in tax avoidance!

Expressions to learn: *Ich liebe meinen Steuerberater!* (I love my tax adviser!)

Avoid saying: Would you mind paying my bill in cash?

39 EMPLOYMENT

Capitalism is often said to be slanted against the interests of the employees, as the employers are usually much more powerful economically. For this reason, the founding fathers of the Federal Republic of Germany were at pains to make Germany a "social market economy". Amongst other things, employees have a lot to say in the running of a firm. In smaller companies, they elect a committee to represent the interests of the employees and in larger companies, they have an even greater influence, since they have the right to 50% of the seats on the company's supervising board.

In addition, employees have considerable protection under employment law. For example, after a maximum of a six months' probationary period, it is almost impossible to fire an employee. When an employee leaves the company, he or she is entitled to a detailed reference, which by law must not contain any negative remarks. Employers have, therefore, invented phrases that sound positive but which other employers will know really mean quite the opposite! For example, the remark that Herr XX "always did his best to carry out his tasks to our full satisfaction", means that he tried but failed! It is wonderful what inventive minds can achieve!

Expressions to learn: *Arbeit bringt das Geld, das Wochenende den Spaß!* (Work brings the money, the weekend the fun!)

Avoid saying: Is there a way of murdering my boss without being caught?

When somebody leaves a job in Germany, they are entitled to a reference from their employer that cannot be negative!

40 SCHOOL

The exact rules for when children have to start school vary from one federal state to another but generally a child must start school at the beginning of the school year (the Autumn) of the year in which it has its sixth birthday. This means that some children don't start school until they are nearly seven, which is quite old by international standards.

Contrary to the practice in most countries, school does not begin at the same time each day but varies from class to class and from day to day. The first lesson can be as early as 7:30 am and on most days at junior school, the last lesson finishes by 12:30 pm. This means that the school day can be quite short but children are given homework every day from their very first day at school and the parents are expected to help them with this. One might, therefore, have the impression that teaching is a part-time job. However, most teachers work long hours preparing for lessons and marking homework and tests outside normal school hours. The real problem is that for years there has been a severe shortage of teachers prepared to teach today's ill-disciplined children!

A child's very first school day is celebrated in style. As some compensation for having to spend the next 12 years enduring boring lessons, children receive a huge cone full of "goodies" when they start school and are the centre of attraction for a day.

Expressions to learn: *Es ist schlimm aber in der Schule musst Du das machen was die Lehrerin sagt!* (It's awful but at school you must do what the teacher says!)

Avoid saying: In my days there was at least some discipline at school!

Children can't start school in Germany until they are strong enough to carry one of those cones full of goodies that they receive on their first school day!

41 UNIVERSITY

In common with most other developed countries, the percentage of school-leavers in Germany going on to higher education constantly increases and reached 50% in the academic year 2017/2018.

For most university courses, attendance at lectures is not compulsory and students can decide themselves when they want to take examinations. Perhaps this is one reason why 30% of those who start a course for a bachelor's degree do not complete it. At most German universities, one is primarily an individual and is not integrated into university life, for example by belonging to societies or playing sport for a university team, as is usual in many other countries.

The average standards of both general and further education vary from one federal state to another. In respect of university degrees, it is usually the faculty concerned that sets standards, so these vary considerably too.

When one is awarded a doctorate, it officially becomes part of the surname in Germany, something usually reserved for medical doctors in many other countries. Having a PhD gives considerable status and Germany has the third highest number of PhD holders globally. However, the desire to have a PhD has led to many accusations of plagiarism in recent years. As a result, even some government ministers have been stripped of their PhD's!

Expressions to learn: *Meine Dissertation war wirklich 100% eigener Arbeit!* (My dissertation was really 100% my own work)!

Avoid asking: Where can I buy a doctorate?

42 NATIONAL PRIDE

The after-effects of the period of National Socialism can hardly be overseen in Germany in one respect, as most Germans are still reluctant to show much pride in their country. There was even a huge public debate in 2002 as to whether one may be proud of being German. Many, including some government ministers, considered it inappropriate to be proud! Even the German national anthem is rarely sung with much enthusiasm, quite in contrast to most other national anthems, except the Spanish one, which is understandable, as it has no words!

Unfortunately, many of the traditional songs praising the German homeland were taken over by the Nazis and are today either banned or people are shy of singing them. However, perhaps the British should rethink whether they should go on singing "Rule Britannia", as this includes the words "Britannia Rules the Waves", something far removed from the truth these days. The anthem also goes on to claim that "Britons never, never, never shall be slaves". However, that was before most young people became slaves to their cell phones!

Most German politicians try to persuade us that in Europe we should forget nationalities and simply regard ourselves as Europeans. Theoretically, this could happen one day when Eurospeak replaces national languages but for the present it is just a dream, comparable with believing that the Euro will survive long-term!

Phrases to learn: *Ich bin stolz Europäer zu sein.* (I'm proud to be a European!)

Avoid saying: And you're really not allowed to be proud of being German?

43 USEFUL IDIOMS (1)

Every country has strange idioms, which when translated literally make little sense. The cartoons on the opposite pages show the picture conjured up by a literal translation into English. The real meanings are explained below:

He has hairs on his teeth! (*Er hat Haare auf den Zähnen!*). He has a sharp tongue.

I press the thumbs for you. (*Ich drücke Dir die Daumen*). I'll keep my fingers crossed for you.

He has tomatoes on his eyes. (*Er hat Tomaten auf den Augen*). He's oblivious to what's going on.

I only understand railway station and departure! (*Ich verstehen nur Bahnhof und Abfahrt!*) It's as clear as mud!

He always goes with his head through the wall. (*Er geht immer mit dem Kopf durch die Wand*). He is always like a bull in a china shop.

He spoke until his mouth frayed! (*Er hat den Mund fransig geredet!*) He talked until he was blue in the face!

Useful Idioms 1

He has hair on
his teeth

I press the thumbs for you!

He has tomatoes
on the eyes.

I understand only railway station
and departure.

He always goes with his
head through the wall.

He spoke until his
mouth frayed.

44 USEFUL IDIOMS (2)

It is amazing how many idioms languages have and, in some cases, it is difficult to imagine how they came about. For example:

I have the nose full. (*Ich habe die Nase voll*). I'm fed up.

Sorry, I'm standing on the hosepipe. (*Entschuldigung, ich stehe auf dem Schlauch*). Sorry, I've thought about it but I just can't understand it.

I had a pig. (*Ich hatte Schwein*). I had a stroke of luck.

I fell with the door in the house. (*Ich bin mit der Tür in das Haus gefallen*). I went at it like a bull at a gate.

I pulled out the legs for you. (*Ich habe die Beine für Dich ausgerissen*). I did everything I could for you.

I'm holding the ears stiff. (*Ich halte die Ohren steif*). I'm keeping my fingers crossed.

Useful Idioms 2

I have my nose full.

Sorry, I am standing on the hosepipe.

I had pig.

I fell with the door into the house.

I pulled out the legs for you.

I'm holding the ears stiff.

45 USEFUL IDIOMS (3)

After living so long in Germany and speaking and writing German daily, I am surprised at I so often still come across idioms I previously didn't know. My selection in this book is from the more common ones, for example:

He took me on the arm. (*Er hat mich auf den Arm genommen.)* He misled me.

He put his finger in the wound! (*Er hat den Finger in die Wunde gelegt!*). He explained where the problem lies.

He has a plank in front of his head! *(Er hat ein Brett vorm Kopf).* He is isn't capable of understanding it.

He makes himself into an ape. (*Er macht sich zum Affen!*). He makes a fool of himself.

You can take poison on it. (*Du kannst Gift darauf nehmen*). You can bet your life on it.

He doesn't have all his cups in the cupboard. (*Er hat nicht alle Tassen im Schrank*). He has a screw loose.

Useful idioms 3

He took me on the arm.

He put his finger in the wound.

He has a plank in front of his head.

He makes himself into an ape.

You can take poison on it.

He doesn't have all his cups in the cupboard.

46 DEPARTURE

Now it's time for you to return home. The flight should have departed at least an hour ago but, as usual at Frankfurt, Germany's largest airport, all flights are delayed because of the long queues at the security checks. The trade union, to which the security people belong, insists that the coffee breaks must be taken as soon as they are due, no matter how long the queues! But think positively - you now have time for a final delicious German beer, although it costs about 50% more than anywhere else in the country.

It's a pity about having to pay for all that excess baggage but your daughter will be delighted with the beautiful traditional dress from Bavaria. However, I'm not so sure how keen your son will be to put on those short *Lederhosen*. Those beer mugs were also probably a waste of money, as British beer doesn't quite taste the same in earthenware. You will probably throw away the cuckoo clock you bought in the Black Forest when you realise how often it wakes you up in the night and you will certainly be disappointed at how quickly your bottle of schnapps seems to empty itself.

At least you could make use of your time waiting to board in trying to learn more of that German grammar, although you have found out that most Germans speak English anyway. Those who don't, will be pleased that you're even trying to speak their language.

Return soon - *auf Wiedersehen*!

An Insider's Guide To Germany

John Morgan

Assisted by Benno Beck

Cartoons by Hannes Mercker, based on ideas from

John Morgan

www.ingramcontent.com/pod-product-compliance
Lightning Source LLC
Chambersburg PA
CBHW051217150426
R18143100001BA/R181431PG42813CBX00014BA/15